Virtuous Woman

Rev Stella Adekunle

Jesus Joy Publishing

Published and printed in Great Britain in 2016 by Jesus Joy Publishing, a division of Eklegein Ltd.

© Stella Adekunle, 2016

All rights reserved. The author gives permission for brief extracts from this book to be used in other publications provided that the following citation is stated:

Extract from 'Virtuous Woman' by Stella Adekunle, 2016; Jesus Joy Publishing, used by permission.

Unless otherwise denoted all scripture quotations are taken from New American Standard Bible ®. Copyright © 1960, 1962, 1963, 1968, 1971, 1972, 1973, 1975, 1977, 1995 by The Lockman Foundation, used by permission.

Scriptures denoted NKJV are taken from New King James Version. Copyright © 1979, 1980, 1982 by Thomas Nelson, Inc., used by permission. All rights reserved.

Scriptures denoted KJV are taken from King James Version. 1611 original, 1769 revision. Crown Copyright.

ISBN 978-1-90797-148-8

Jesus Joy Publishing
A division of Eklegein Ltd
www.jesusjoypublishing.co.uk
20160816

Acknowledgment

Glory be to God in the highest for His faithfulness towards everyone of us. I give thanks, honour and adoration to the name of our Lord Jesus Christ who has made it possible to complete this book. The bible says - *"Not by might nor by power but by My Spirit says the Lord of host."* [Zechariah 4:6]

I appreciated the anointing of the Holy Spirit that has given the inspiration through the write up of each topic.

Once again, I give thanks to the Lord for He is good, for His mercy endures forever.

Rev Stella Adekunle
Sword of the Spirit Evangelical Outreach
www.sseooutreach.org.uk

Contents

3	Acknowledgment
15	Helpers Comparable Part 1
39	Helpers Comparable Part 2
49	Glorious Women to the Family and Nation
57	Women of Great Wisdom
71	Warriors for the Kingdom
91	The Power of Women
105	Women of Great Faith
119	Women as Vehicles of Restoration
127	Victorious Women
135	Devoted Women
143	Women's Position as Mothers
153	Women's Position in the House of God
163	Women's Position in the Community
171	Keys to becoming a Virtuous Woman
183	Women's Customs, Culture and Fashion
191	Also By The Author

Introduction

Introduction

The word 'virtuous' conveys the following qualities:

> *Righteous, good, moral, ethical upright, high minded, right thinking, principled, exemplary, clean, law abiding, lawful, irreproachable, blameless, guiltless, unimpeachable, just, honest, honourable un-bribe-able, incorruptible, ant-corruption.*

Therefore, to be qualified to be called virtuous, a woman must be of high moral standing and who lives according to biblical standards in a compromised society.

The virtuous woman is an embodiment of the ideal attitude and characteristics of what the woman of yesterday, today and tomorrow should be. The Word of God explains the role of women in the church of God, at home and in the community. It acknowledges the work of great women and the qualities they possessed that made them great. It highlights women such as:

- Sarah, who called her husband *"lord"* due to her obedient and humbled nature, *"as Sarah obeyed Abraham calling him lord, whose daughters you are if you do good and are not afraid with terror."* [1 Peter 3:6]

- Ruth, who was faithful to Naomi her mother in-law even after the death of her husband.

- Abigail, who delivered her household from sudden death by applying God's wisdom in her life.

- Deborah, the warrior woman, who saved the people of Israel in battle with Jabin king of Syria.

- Queen Esther, the woman of integrity, who saved a whole generation from the hand of Haman.

This book examines the ills in the society concerning women and points out the keys to becoming a successful wife/mother. This scriptural work explores the characteristics of a unique woman both at home and outside the four walls.

Chapter 1

Helpers Comparable Part 1

> *"And the Lord said, it is not good that man should be alone, I will make him a helper comparable* [another Bible version states, *"a helper fit"*] *to him."*
>
> [Genesis 2:18]

This verse reveals the primary intention of God for creating a woman. The primary purpose of God for every woman is to be a helper in every way to her husband. God's original intention for men and women was that they be united in matrimony and bear children; however, in our fallen world, this plan is often subverted. Before God created a helper fit for Adam, He created different types of animals but none of them could serve the purpose or the intention of God in finding a fitting companion for the man.

> *"Out of the ground the Lord God formed every beast of the field and every bird of the air, and brought them to Adam to see what he would*

call them. And whatever Adam called each living creature, that was its name. So Adam gave names to all cattle, to the birds of the air, and to every beast of field, but for Adam there was not found a helper comparable to him."

[Genesis 2:19-20]

Therefore, God made a female out of man and Adam named her Eve:

"And the Lord God caused a deep sleep to fall on Adam, and he slept, and He took one of his ribs, and closed up the flesh its place. Then the rib which the Lord had taken from man He made into a woman, and He brought her to the man. And Adam said ...she shall be called woman."

[Genesis 2:21-23]

God created woman to fill an important vacancy in the life of a man; Eve fulfilled this role with only one recorded shortcoming. She was the one who first ate the forbidden fruit which God commanded them not to eat:

> "So when the woman saw that the tree was good for food, that it was pleasant to the eyes, and a tree desirable to make one wise, she took of its fruit and ate. She also gave to her husband with her and he ate."
> [Genesis 3:6]

Eve was created to be a helper for Adam in the garden and not the decision- maker. Even though the Bible indicates that Adam was with her, there is no record that he did or said anything to prevent Eve from eating the forbidden fruit. This is why God held Adam accountable for Eve's deception. Nevertheless, Eve took the position of a man in the affairs of the home rather than being a helper fit for the man. This caused her lots of pains and troubles, which were passed down to the whole of mankind.

> "...'I will greatly multiply your sorrow and your conception; in pain you shall

> *bring forth children; your desire shall be for your husband, and he shall rule over you.' Then to Adam He said, '... because you have heeded the voice of your wife, and have eaten from the tree... cursed is the ground for your sake; in toil you shall eat of it all the days of your life...In the sweat of your face you shall eat bread till you return to the ground... for dust you are, and to dust you shall return'."*
>
> [Genesis 3:16-19]

However, human beings were created initially to live comfortably in the garden and to reflect the glory of God and nothing else:

> *"Everyone who is called by my name who I have created for My glory, I have formed him, I have made him."*
>
> [Isaiah 43:7]

But because of the sin committed in the garden by Adam and Eve, humanity lost the opportunities and the right to reflect the glory of God which was the primary intent of God for creating them in His own image.

The spiritual consequences were that God separated Himself from mankind, and the death sentence was passed on whoever dies in his or her sin. *"... for the wages of sin is death..."* [Roman 6:23] And physically God separated from Adam and Eve by not visiting them in person as was His habit before the Fall. They lost the boldness of approaching God in their lives and the spirit of fear came upon Adam and Eve so that when they heard God coming they ran to hid themselves:

> *"... and they heard the sound of the Lord God walking in the garden in the cool of the day, and Adam and his wife hid themselves from the presence of the Lord God among the trees of the garden."*
> [Genesis 3:8]

Adam and Eve went so far as to hide themselves amongst the trees. They trusted in the trees and chose them as a cover for themselves.

Perhaps if Adam and Eve had taken the step of repentance and asking for forgiveness before God visited them, things would have been different today:

> *"If we confess our sins, He is faithful and just to forgive us our sins and to cleanse us from all unrighteousness."*
>
> [1 John 1:9]

Now, do a personal assessment of yourself and consider the following questions:

- In what ways are you not fulfilling the purpose of God for your life?

- In what ways have you allowed your sins to drive you away from the presence of the Lord God and how far have these sins driven you?

- Do you also trust in idols as your saviour in time of trouble?

- What is your preferred idol?

- Where do you hide whenever you sin against God?

- In what ways have you allowed the sins in your life to drive away the Holy Spirit who is the light to your path?

- When you commit sin and the Holy Spirit chastises you, what do you do? Do you repent and ask for forgiveness from God or do you ignore it and carry on as if nothing has happened?

- In what ways have you undermined your husband which may have led to disasters into your marriage?

Please take the opportunity today to repent. As a virtuous woman, you are supposed to be a builder and not a destroyer. Physically, the punishment of God followed the sin of disobedience in the garden of Eden, and if God did not spare the first creation, then He will not spare us either.

If God did not show partiality even to the angel, then why should we think He will show partiality to us? The Bible states:

> *"For if God did not spare the angels who sinned, but cast them down to hell and delivered them into chains of darkness, to be reserved for judgement and did not spare the ancient world but saved Noah, one of the eight people, a preacher of righteousness, bringing in the flood on the world of the ungodly and turning the cities of Sodom and Gomorrah into ashes, condemned them to destruction, making them an example to those who afterward would live ungodly…"*
> [2 Peter 2:4-6]

Re-assess your behaviour and make necessary corrections in whatever way you have failed to be in the position God has ordained you to be as 'a helper fit' for your husband. In situations where he may not be walking in his role as head of the home, the wife may be tempted to take over the leadership. If you have ever taken over the position as head of the family from your husband, please go right now before God and ask for forgiveness; then approach your husband to work things out. Let him know that you made the mistake out of ignorance and promise not to repeat it, but to become a virtuous woman:

> "The wise woman builds her house, but the foolish pulls it down with her hands."
>
> [Proverbs 14:1]

The Bible makes it clear that Adam sinned whilst Eve was deceived. So, it is Adam whom God held accountable as the head of the home:

> "... then to Adam He said, 'Because you have heeded the voice of your wife, and have eaten from the tree of which I commanded you, saying, -You shall not eat of it: " Cursed is the ground for your

> *sake; In toil you shall eat of it all the days of your life."*
>
> [Genesis 3:17]

Probably if their rebellion in the garden had not happened, human beings would not have been dying and returning to dust. According to the Scriptures, our God is immortal and man is created in God's image :

> *"So God created man in His own image, in the image of God He created Him, male and female He created them."*
>
> [Genesis 1:27]

Characteristics of a helper fit for the man

Let us consider this checklist found in king Solomon's description of the virtuous wife in Proverbs 31:10-31. We will focus on the aspects of her character which can apply to all woman as emphasised below.

Who can find **a virtuous wife?** For her

worth is far above rubies.

The heart of her husband safely trusts her; so he will have no lack of gain.

She does him good and not evil all the days of her life.

She seeks wool and flax, and **willingly works with her hands**.

She is like the merchant ships, she brings her food from afar.

She also rises while it is yet night, and provides food for her household, and a portion for her maidservants.

She considers a field and buys it; from her profits she plants a vineyard.

She girds herself with strength, and strengthens her arms.

She perceives that her merchandise *is* good, and her lamp does not go out by night.

She stretches out her hands to the distaff, and her hand holds the spindle.

She extends her hands to the poor, yes, she reaches out her hands to the needy.

She is not afraid of snow for her household, for all her household *is* clothed with scarlet.

She makes tapestry for herself; her clothing *is* fine linen and purple.

Her husband is known in the gates, when he sits among the elders of the land.

She makes linen garments and sells them, and supplies sashes for the merchants.

Strength and honour are her clothing; she shall rejoice in time to come.

She opens her mouth with wisdom, and on her tongue is the law of kindness.

She watches over the ways of her household, and **does not eat the bread of idleness**.

Her children rise up and call her blessed; her husband *also,* and he praises her: *"Many daughters have done well, but you excel them all."*

Charm *is* deceitful and beauty *is* passing, but a woman who fears the LORD, she shall be praised.

Give her of the fruit of her hands, and let her own works praise her in the gates.

Let us explain some of these characteristics emphasised in the above passage.

Honourable:

A *"helper fit"* should be a woman of honour for her own sake as well as her husband's. In whatever situation she finds herself, her actions and attitudes should portray her as a woman of integrity. She should take delight in her family and never bring shame to her husband:

"Her husband is known in the gates when he sits among the elders of the land."
[Proverbs 31:23]

Let us consider what Peter says about such a woman:

Do not let your adornment be merely outward- arranging the hair, wearing gold, or putting on fine apparel - rather let it be the hidden person of the heart, with the incorruptible beauty of a gentle and quiet spirit, which is very precious in the sight of God.
[1 Peter 3:3-4]

Efficient and Effective:

A *"helper fit"* must be a dutiful and efficient woman yet willing to humble herself to God and to her husband:

> *"She watches over the ways of her household, and she does not eat the bread of idleness."*
>
> [Proverbs 31:27]

She must be able to coordinate the home affairs with total and loving submission to her husband. That some women suffer in silence in their matrimonial home by a bullying husband should not be mistaken for biblical submission as outlined in Ephesians 5:22-25. For example, some women take it upon themselves to furnish the house with a bank loan but without consulting their husbands. It is not wrong to help their husbands but it must be an agreement between the two. Her efficiency and effectiveness must not be taken as a liberty to dominate and suppress her husband.

She must be able to combine the following roles together and perform them simultaneously be:

- a doctor in case of minor accidents at home,

- a teacher and guardian to the children,

- a director of the affairs in the kitchen,

- a comforter for her husband in times of distress,

- a disciplinarian to the children.

She must be very strong and not a lazy type. She must be ready to work and earn money to help support her husband and children if necessary. However, not every woman needs to work outside the home; it all depends on the family income and what the husband and wife agree is best for them. Some couples decide that the wife will be a stay-at-home mum or home-maker as her occupation.

Kindly note that working to support the husband in the home does not mean working to take control of the home. A wife must be prepared to support her husband in whatever way is necessary- financially, by going out to work, spiritually, by fasting and praying for the progress of the family; and physically, by keeping the home clean and tidy at all times. [Proverbs 31:15-16]

Prayerful:

She must be a prayer warrior. A woman needs to be ready to stand in the gap for her family at all times, and to use her committed relationship with God to make changes in her husband's and children's lives. She must be willing to pray until something good happens in the event of trouble and problems in the family.

Generous:

She gives alms to the poor and needy and this is rewarding not only here on earth but also in heaven *"... and her lamp does not goes out by night (prayer) ... she extends her hand to the poor, yes she reaches out her hand to the needy"* [Proverbs 31:18-20]

Exemplary:

A *"helper fit"* must be a woman who is ready to work for God, and able to inspire others through her attitude to her husband and people in her surroundings. She has the love of the lost sheep at heart and is willing to go after them to win them for Christ. She is an excellent woman who through her way of life will be an example to, and challenge other women to make a difference in their homes and community as a whole:

"... she opens her mouth with wisdom, and on her tongue is the law of kindness... Her children rise up and call her blessed; her husband also, and he praises her; Many daughters have done well, but you excel them all."

[Proverbs 31:26-29]

Respectable:

A *"helper fit"* must be a woman of good reputation within and outside the home. She will not bring shame and disgrace to the family or tarnish the image of her family. She will always be a good ambassador of her household. Her desire will always be to bring glory and honour to the family:

> *"She makes linen garments and sells them, and supplies sashes for the merchants. Strength and honour are her clothing."*
>
> [Proverbs 31:24-25]

God-fearing:

She must respect and honour God first in all her undertakings. All her conduct must reflect the fear of God and she will only achieve this by living according to the will of God in her household and in the community at large:

> "Charm is deceitful and beauty is passing, but a woman who fears the Lord, she shall be praised."
>
> [Proverbs 31:30]

Teachable:

She must be ready to follow God's directions through the Holy Spirit and willingly accept the instructions given by her husband. She must submit totally to the control and authority of her husband not as a slave but in love and in line with the Word of God. For example, if your husband asks you to become a prostitute in order to earn money to feed the household, you must refuse to commit such a sin. After all, does it befit the child of God to engage in harlotry and will God be proud of you when He sees you?

Since your answer must be **No,** then you must prayerfully refuse such instruction.

"... wives, likewise be submissive to your

husbands, that even if some do not obey the word, they without a word, may be won by the conduct of their wives."

[1 Peter 3:1]

Trustworthy:

She must be a woman whom her husband can trust in all matters, and who will never betray his trust. She is ready to go to any length in order to make her husband happy whenever it is necessary but only in the will of God. She will always receive her husband with open arms even when he is at fault and correct him in love. Many women have lost the trust of their husbands because they harbour resentment in relation to the mistakes revealed to them by their husbands and then use these against their husbands when any little misunderstanding arises at home.

For example, a man came home late from work because of his female manager who insisted that he accompany her to the supermarket. The man told his wife the cause of his lateness and since then his wife has used it to attack him each time he comes home late. Such a woman will lose her husband's trust and her attitude will only predispose him towards telling lies instead of the truth.

Take time to meditate on this guiding principle:

> *"The heart of her husband safely trusts her, so he will have no lack of gain. She does him good and not evil all the days of her life."*
>
> [Proverbs 31:11-12]

Chapter 2

Helpers Comparable Part 2

In this chapter, we will consider the attributes of a woman who is far from the purpose of God. The plan of God for women is to be helpers who are fit for their husbands but in the case of a woman like Jezebel, she was the opposite - a helper fit for destruction. She conspired with her husband to get the garden of Naboth by arranging for his murder simply because he refused to sell his property to the king. The Bible records:

> *"... she wrote letters in Ahab's name, and sealed them with his seal, and sent the letters unto the elders and to the nobles that were in his city, dwelling with Naboth and she wrote in the letters, saying, Proclaim a fast, and set Naboth on high among the people and set two men, sons of Belial, before him, to bear witness against him, saying, Thou didst blaspheme God and the king and then carry him out, and stone him, that he may*

> die."
>
> [1 Kings 21:8-10]

She was highly possessed with evil spirits and had different shrines and altars on which she operated and a lot of followers. She not only brought curses upon her husband [1 Kings 21:21-22] but also contributed to the suspension of the ministry of prophet Elijah by causing fear and intimidation to cause him to run for his life and want to die:

> *"Then Jezebel sent a messenger unto Elijah, saying, So let the gods do to me, and more also, if I make not thy life as the life of one of them by tomorrow about this time and when he saw that, he arose, and went for his life, and came to Beer-sheba, which belongeth to Judah, and left his servant there. But he himself went a day's journey into the wilderness, and came and sat down under a juniper tree: and he requested for himself that he might die; and said, It is enough; now, O LORD, take away my life; for I am not better than my*

> *fathers."*
>
> [1 Kings 19:2-4]

Delilah was another woman in the scripture who took part in an evil contract to terminate the ministry of Samson:

> *"... it came to pass afterward, that he loved a woman in the valley of Sorek, whose name was Delilah and the lords of the Philistines came up unto her, and said unto her, 'Entice him, and see wherein his great strength lieth, and by what means we may prevail against him, that we may bind him to afflict him: and we will give thee every one of us eleven hundred pieces of silver.'"*
>
> [Judges 16:4-5]

She succeeded in her evil plans and Samson was captured by his enemies through his lover. The account reads as follows:

> *"... then she lulled him to sleep on her knees, and called for a man and had him*

> *shave off the seven locks of his head. Then she began to torment him, and his strength left him. And she said, "The Philistines are upon you, Samson!" So he awoke from his sleep, and said, "I will go out as before, at other times, and shake myself free!" But he did not know that the LORD had departed from him. Then the Philistines took him and put out his eyes, and brought him down to Gaza. They bound him with bronze fetters, and he became a grinder in the prison."*
>
> [Judges 16:19-21]

In both cases, even though they were pagan women and thus not subject to the law and purposes of God, they did not help the men they claimed to love but rather contributed to their destruction. They were filled with the spirit of covetousness, lusted after possessions and were seducers. They were *"... lovers of pleasure more than lovers of God."* [2 Timothy 3:4]

Now is time to determine whether you are

operating in the same spirit as these women or not. Consider the following questions and answer, honestly, *Yes* or *No* to each and keep a score:

- Do you love your husband conditionally - except where he asks you to do something outside of God's Word?

- Do you easily get angry with him?

- Do you prefer the company of others to that of your husband?

- Is there any hidden secret that you would rather tell another person and not your husband?

- Would you obey your husband rather than God because of your love for your husband?

- Would you do anything for your husband in order to achieve his goal in life even if it involves committing sin?

- Would you sell your body for pleasure or monetary purpose through prostitution?

- Do you only look your best whenever you want some favour or things done by your husband?

- Do you prefer satisfaction provided by outsiders to that of your family?

Be honest with yourself in answering the above questions. They are designed to help you know who you are and to make necessary corrections before it is too late.

If your 'Yes' score is above five, then you are likely to have the spirit of Jezebel and Delilah.

If you fall below five, congratulations but still strive to work on your weaknesses. This is not to condemn anyone for we all have weaknesses. It is not how many times you fall that counts but how you recover from your falls.

Chapter 3

Glorious Women to the Family and Nation

"The wise woman builds her house, but the foolish pulls it down with her hands."
[Proverbs 14:1]

A *"helper fit"* for her husband will build her home not with bricks and mortar but with the word and wisdom of God. But a foolish woman will pull down even the one that has been built. An example of a foolish woman who pulled down rather than built her home was Vashti, the wife of king Ahasuerus. This queen was a beautiful lady and a prominent woman of her time. Queen Vashti's beauty was so remarkable that her husband liked to show her off to his visitors in the palace. One day the king hosted an official feast for his servants and distinguished guests from his neighbourhood. The king requested his wife's presence to show off her beauty as usual to entertain his guests but queen Vashti refused. [Esther 1:10-11] The queen did not only disrespect and disgrace her husband but the nation as a whole because the feast was for the officials in the kingdom. The king was greatly annoyed and dethroned Vashti from being his wife and queen of the land.

The Bible states that:

> *"the wise shall inherit glory but shame shall be the legacy or promotion of fools".*
> [Proverbs 3:35]

Queen Vashti was wise in her own eyes and her wisdom was shown to be folly. A virtuous woman will always seek to please and honour her husband but Vashti's arrogant attitude brought destruction and downfall to her. Pride made her lose her position as wife and queen of her nation.

What about you? Are you too proud to submit to your husband. Take this opportunity to search your heart and resolve to mend your ways before God because:

> *"Pride goes before destruction, And a haughty spirit before a fall"*
>
> [Proverbs 16:18]

Because the Bible states:

> *"... exaltation comes neither from the east nor from the west nor from the south, but God is the Judge He puts down one, and exalts another."*
>
> [Psalm 75:6-7]

God promoted a slave girl from obscurity to the palace, from nowhere to the highest level in her nation. God exalted Esther to the position of Queen of the land. It was Esther's exaltation that brought victory to her people, the Jews. Indeed, there is always a purpose for any step a righteous person takes. In other words, there is always a purpose for any step that God permit us to take. As a virtuous woman, learn how to humble yourself and make yourself available for God to use. Despite the fact that Esther was a slave, she did not forget God and He eventually uplifted her. We are told that queen Esther was a devoted wife of king Ahasrueus, and that she humbled herself and obeyed all the rules of the palace. When the time came to decide how to proceed, to stand up for her people, she broke one of the rules in the palace. However, she fasted and prayed for God's favour beforehand, and came back victoriously.

Let us consider some good qualities in Esther's life that contributed to her success:

- Esther was a virgin girl before her night with the king, and subsequent promotion to the position of queen.

"... then the king's servants who attended him said: 'let beautiful young virgins be sought for the king.'"

[Esther 2:2]

- God cherishes undefiled souls, because a sinner cannot see the glory of God:

"... now we know that God does not hear the sinners; but if anyone is a worshipper of God and does His will, He hears him."

[John 9:31]

- She received favour from the king and was chosen as the queen. This could not be achieved without her fervent prayer. It is my belief that during the month of her preparation before her appearance in the palace, she must have prayed and lived a sanctified life:

"... the king loved Esther more than all the other woman, and she obtained grace and favour in sight more than all the virgins; so he set his royal crown upon her head and made her queen instead of Vashti."

[Esther 2:17]

- She kept to the commandment of her uncle Mordecai by not revealing her identity:

"Esther had not revealed her people or

family, for Mordecai had charged her not to reveal it."

[Esther 2:1]

- She humbled herself to Mordecai's authority and followed the advice of her custodian in the palace, Hegai:

"... she requested nothing but what Hegai, the king's eunuch, the custodian of the women, advised. And Esther obtained favour in the sight of all who saw her."

[Esther 2:15]

Chapter 4

Women of Great Wisdom

"The fear of the Lord is the beginning of wisdom, and the knowledge of the Holy one is understanding."

[Proverbs 9:10]

The previous chapter made us aware that women who are full of wisdom and fear God will build their own homes but the foolish ones will destroy them:

"The wise woman builds her house, but the foolish pulls it down with her hands."

[Proverbs 14:1]

There are many examples of this in the scripture but under this heading we shall look at experiences from the lives of two great women who by their action saved the lives of their families.

Abigail was a woman of great wisdom according to the scripture:

> *"The name of the man was Nabal, and the name of his wife Abigail: she was a woman of good understanding and beautiful in appearance, but he was harsh and evil in his doings."*
>
> [1 Samuel 25:3]

Abigail's wise action saved her household because Nabal's ingratitude toward David would have cost the lives of every male of the family. And where there is no male in the family there will be no continuity in the genealogy of the family. Since Nabal was a wealthy man, David sent a request to share some provisions with him and his men:

> *"... let my young men find favour in your eyes, for we come on a feast day please give whatever comes to your hand to your servant and to your son David."*
>
> [1 Samuel 25:8]

As if Nabal's refusal wasn't bad enough, he also insulted David's heritage:

> *"Who is David and who is son of Jesse?...
> shall I then take my bread and water and
> my meat that I have killed for my shearers,
> and give it to men when I do not know
> where they are from?"*
> [1 Samuel 25:10-11]

Though David was not as wealthy as Nabal, he had power and weapons of war. Therefore when David heard this, he commanded his servant to prepare for war against Nabal:

> *"Then David said to his men, every man gird on his sword."*
> [1 Samuel 25:13]

The news of what David was about to do reached Abigail through one of the young men that visited Nabal on behalf of David to deliver his message. Abigail used the divine wisdom deposited in her to intervene and nip David's hostility in the bud.

The Bible states:

> *"... then Abigail made haste and she took two hundred loaves of bread, two skins of wine, five seahs of roasted grain, one hundred clusters of raisins, and two hundred cakes of figs and loaded them on the donkey. And she said to her servants, go on before me; see I am coming after you. But she did not tell her husband Nabal."*
>
> [1 Samuel 25:18-19]

Let's focus on the boldness of Abigail's action. She did not tell her husband because she knew that he would disallow her from going to see David which would have led to David's destruction of Nabal. It is important to note that Abigail's secret action does not mean that she disobeyed her husband by taking matters into her own hands and going to David without informing her husband. There are some sacrifices a virtuous woman will make to save her family from destruction.

Women often have special gifts to see things

afar off before they happen while men tend to focus on immediate things. Women prepare in advance to prevent evil future occurrences but men deal with immediate problems without second thought. Abigail knew that her husband was a drunkard and so was not capable of rational thinking; furthermore, she saw the evil that would follow her husband's refusal to give David the share he requested:

> *"... may God do so, and more also, to the enemies of David, if I leave one male of all who belong to him by morning light."*
> [1 Samuel 25:22]

But Nabal only saw the financial loss which he would suffer by giving the food to David.

> *"... shall I then take my bread and water and my meat that I have killed for my shearers, and give it to men when I do not know where they are from?"*
> [1 Samuel 25:11]

There is an idiomatic expressions - 'a stitch in time saves nine'. In a situation like this, a virtuous woman does not need to ask for permission from her husband before she takes a step to rectify mistakes that can cause loss. She does not need to wait for things to get out of hands for the sake of obtaining permission from her husband before she prays and fasts for God to turn the situation around to favour her family. For example, if the husband is away on a business trip and there is an emergency to attend to on his behalf, a virtuous woman must take the risk and sacrifice whatever it takes to spare the family a court case or penalty fine.

A virtuous woman needs to seek to understand her husband, and know where and when to help at his point of need. Do not forget that each man has his own weakness and this is why we are called to be *"a helper fit"* for the purpose, to comfort and console when and where necessary.

"... two are better than one, because if they

> *fall, one will lift up his companion. But woe to him who is alone when he falls for he has no one to help him up."*
>
> [Ecclesiastes 4:9-10]

A virtuous woman needs the wisdom of God at all times in order to avoid making mistakes and taking wrong decisions.

As we continue to grow in the Lord, He will increase our wisdom through our day to day experiences in our homes and community, and widen our knowledge through God's Word. Pray that God will empower you with His divine wisdom and give you the spirit of discernment when necessary. Without this we cannot fulfil the role God expects us to play as virtuous women and helpers fit for our husbands.

Rahab, the harlot, was another woman of wisdom who through her action saved her family when God wanted to destroy Jericho. Who would think that a harlot would be so wise to the extent that the Bible records her as one of the heroes of faith.

> *"... by faith the harlot Rahab did not perish with those who did not believe, when she had received the spies with peace."*
>
> [Hebrew 11:31]

Rahab used the wisdom of God in her life to host the spies sent by Joshua to the land of Jericho during the Israelites journey through the wilderness. Being a harlot, one would have expected her to seduce them and take the opportunity to get them into bed but she did not do this. Instead she took care of them; even when the king sent messengers with the threat of death for any spies, the woman hid them and told the king's messengers that the two men had been with her but had left for an unknown destination. Meanwhile the two men were on top of her roof, and when it was dark she let them down by rope through the window of her house for safety with the instruction on how to escape death:

> *"... and she said to them: 'get to the mountain, lest the pursuers meet you, hide there three days, until the pursers have returned, after that you may go your way.'"*
>
> [Joshua 2:16]

Rahab required the wisdom of God to know what to do and how to advise the spies; without this, the two spies would have been killed without achieving the purpose of their visit to Jericho and the Israelites would have been in darkness concerning the land.

Rehab not only delivered the spies from death through the wisdom of God in her but she made the spies swear to protect her family and thus future generations.

> *"Now therefore, swear to me by the Lord, since I have shown you kindness to my father's house, and give me a true token and spare my father, and mother, my brothers and my sisters and all that they*

> *have, and deliver our lives from death."*
> [Joshua 2:12-14]

Rehab insisted that the spies make this vow to her because: she wanted to be sure of the safety and well-being of her family. Sometimes people forget the past favours we do for them, but God does not. There is also the possibility that a person's circumstances can change and it may no longer be possible to return the favour. Such was the case with Joseph and Pharaoh in the land of Egypt. A new Pharaoh came to the throne and he did not know all that Joseph had done in interpreting the dream of the former Pharaoh, and preventing the Egyptians from dying of hunger during the famine.

> *"... now there arose a new king over Egypt, who did not know Joseph."*
> [Exodus 1:8]

But in the case of Rahab, the spies kept their promise and it came to pass when God was about to destroy Jericho, she and her family were saved:

> "... and they utterly destroyed all that was in the city, both men and woman, young and old, ox and sheep and donkey, with the edge of sword. But Joshua had said to the two men who had spied out the country, Go into the harlot's house, and from there bring out the woman and all that she has, as you swore to her."
>
> [(Joshua 6:21-24]

Rahab did not only request for her own safety but sought to safeguard the rest of her family and consequently generations to come. This reflects the character of a virtuous woman. A virtuous woman must always seek the peace of her household. Through the wisdom of God in her, she will be able to turn situations around for good. She needs to study and understand her husband and know when and where her quick action is necessary in order to rescue the family from a terrible outcome as was the case with

Nabal and Abigail. Finally, if you want to be a prayer warrior, you must be ready and willing to pray until you get a result or reassurance that God has answered you even though it may not yet be visible. Pray now for the divine wisdom and discernment from God that will help you to obtain all the listed qualities and to succeed as a wife and mother at home.

> *"How much better to get wisdom than gold! And to get understanding is to be chosen rather than silver."*
>
> *[Proverbs 16:16]*

Chapter 5

Warriors for the Kingdom

> *"Put on the whole armour of God, that you may be able to stand against the wiles of the devil. For we do not wrestle against flesh and blood, but against principalities, against powers, against the rulers of the darkness of this age, against spiritual hosts of wickedness in the heavenly places."*
>
> [Ephesians 6:11-12]

From these verses, it is clear that the Christian's warfare is not carnal which means it is not a battle where we can fight with weapons of war such as missiles, guns, bows and arrows, or wrestle as the wrestlers on the sports stage. Because it is a spiritual battle, we cannot see our opponents with ordinary eyes but only with the inner eyes of God.

> *"... wisdom is in the sight of him who has understanding, but the eyes of a fool are*

> *on the ends of the earth."*
> [Proverbs 17:24]

The battlefield is the heart of man, and most weapons the enemies, powers and principalities, use are through attacking us in our dreams by sowing seeds of evil thoughts. An example of a spiritual battle in the dream is being shot in the dream at a particular part of body and then waking up with a pain on the spot.

> *"... the heart is deceitful above all things, and desperately wicked; who can know it?"*
> [Jeremiah 17:9]

A virtuous woman must understand all the weapons of her spiritual warfare and be able to take up the whole armour of God and face both the physical and spiritual battles in her family and all aspects of her life. She needs to be fully aware that the major weapons of her warfare are the Word of God, fasting and prayer.

Jesus Christ, being the example of our spiritual warfare has experienced this before us and has given us the victory in the spiritual realm. Jesus warred against Satan physically and spiritually in the wilderness after His forty days and forty nights of fasting. He was tempted by Satan, it was a battle between Light and Darkness in which Satan used all necessary weapons such as food, position and elevation to tempt Jesus but he failed. The only weapon used by Jesus was the Word of God - *"it is written."* The devil is clever in his own ways, and he also used the Word of God but quoted it wrongly to suit his own purpose which ultimately failed.

Are we using the word of God wrongly? Please examine and correct yourself if necessary for God will never answer such prayers. The gospel of St Luke states:

> *"... now when the devil had ended every temptation, he departed from Him until*

an opportune time."

[Luke 4:13]

Truly Satan departed as he had promised and came back through the afflictions and death of Jesus on the cross where the last battle took place. Jesus Christ fought the battle against death and Hades and finally brought victory to all through His resurrection and ascension.

"Knowing that Christ, having been raised from the dead, dies no more. Death no longer has dominion over Him."

[Roman 6:9]

"Thanks be to God, who gives us the victory through our Lord Jesus Christ."

[1 Corinthians 15:57]

As a warrior woman for God, we are expected to put on the armour of God and stand in the gap with our prayers, fasting and meditating in the Word of God for the people in our family, church and community as a whole.

Deborah is a notable example of a warrior woman in the scriptures. She led and fought the battle, with the support of God, and made a positive impact in the country at that time. She led the army of God against Sisera and conquered.

> *"...if God is for us who can be against us?"*
> *[Roman 8:31]*

Perhaps you have not yet put on the armour of God or you are afraid of war like the man who was commissioned for the purpose but gave the glory of the victory in battle to Deborah because of his cowardliness:

> *"... and Barak said if you will go with me then I will go; but if you will not go with me I will not go!"*
> *[Judge 4:8]*

Deborah agreed to go with him and Barak

lost the glory of the victorious battle to a woman because of fear. So she said:

> *"I will surely go with you; nevertheless there will be no glory for you in the journey you are taking, for the Lord will sell Sisera into the hand of woman."*
>
> [Judges 4:9]

God is looking for women like Deborah in this generation to wage spiritual warfare against the devil and his agents. They must be women who are not afraid to wage war as individuals and corporately with other armies of the Lord during these end times and come back victorious. The battle between Deborah and Sisera was physical but the battle of the children of God in the world today is spiritual; it is not war against flesh and blood since no one can see the devil's warriors according to the scriptures.

> *"... for we do not wrestle against flesh and blood, but against the rulers of the darkness of this age, against spiritual*

> *hosts of wickedness in the heavenly places."*
>
> [Ephesians 6:12]

The Bible describes the arch-enemy of our spiritual warfare as the devil called Satan.

> *"... be sober, be vigilant; because your adversary the devil walks about like a roaring lion, seeking whom he may devour."*
>
> [1 Peter 5:8]

Although the devil is like a lion, though it is Jesus who is the *"Lion of the Tribe of Judah"*. The devil is a toothless lion who has no power to do anything other than to threaten. Do not bow to his intimidation nor give him a foothold in your life.

> *"... neither give place to the devil"*
>
> [Ephesians 4:27]

Do not forget that our battle is of the Lord and He has promised to fight for us. Though it may be very rough and seem as though the end has come, always remember what God said in Exodus:

> *"... the Lord will fight for you and you shall hold your peace."*
>
> [Exodus 14:14]

Notably, Satan left Jesus until an opportune time as recorded by the gospel according to Saint Luke; therefore the children of God will always be at war with Satan and this will only end when we are able to cross the spiritual Jordan to our Heavenly Canaan. There Jesus will wipe away all tears and welcome the overcomers into His kingdom.

> *"... and God will wipe away every tear from their eyes; there shall be no more death, nor sorrow, nor crying. There shall be no more pain, for the former things have passed away."*
>
> [Revelation 21:4]

But until then, the Bible recommends the

following 'battle strategies' for anyone to fight and overcome both physical and spiritual battles in their lives:

- Renew your mind.

    This must be done continuously, so that the devil will not defeat us.

    "... do not be conformed to this world, but be transformed by the renewing of your mind, that you may prove what is that good and acceptable and perfect will of God."
    [Romans 12:2]

    Each time Satan is at work in your heart, learn to use the word of God which is the sword of the Spirit to fight, for it is the greatest weapon to overcome Satan and his angels.

    "Then they cried out to the Lord in their trouble, and He saved them out of their distresses. He sent His word and healed

> *them, and delivered them from their destruction."*
>
> [Psalm 107:19-20]

- Flee from temptation and resist the devil steadfastly.

> *"Blessed is the man who endures temptation; for when he has been approved, he will receive the crown of life which the Lord has promised to those who love Him."*
>
> [James 1:12]

- Put on the full armour of God

> *"Put on the whole armour of God, that you may be able to stand against the wiles of the devil."*
>
> [Ephesians 6:11]

The armour of God consists of the:

Breastplate of righteousness,

Feet with the preparation of the gospel,

Shield of Faith,

Helmet of salvation

Sword of the Spirit which is the Word of God.

Most importantly, you must be 'born again' for if not, all your striving against Satan will be as if you are blowing in the wind. Moreover, the devil cannot fight himself.

> "... he who sins is of the devil, for the devil has sinned from the beginning. For this purpose the Son of God was manifested, that He might destroy the works of the devil. Whoever has been born of God does not sin."
>
> [1 John 3:8-9]

A Prayer Warrior

> "But every woman who prays or prophesies with her head uncovered dishonors her head, for that is one and the same as if her head were shaved. For

> *if a woman is not covered, let her also be shorn. But if it is shameful for a woman to be shorn or shaved, let her be covered."*
>
> [1 Corinthians 11:5-6]

Prayer was one of the major aspects of the weapons of war for the early church. They used prayers to attain the standard or holiness Jesus wanted for them with the power of the Holy Spirit:

> *"... and when they had prayed, the place where they were assembled together was shaken and they were all filled with the Holy Spirit, and they spoke the word of God with boldness."*
>
> [Acts 4:31]

Prayer played an important role and went a long way to assist the Apostles of the early church to achieve what Jesus enacted before His ascension:

> *"... they continued steadfastly in the apostles' doctrine and fellowship, in the*

> *breaking of bread and prayers."*
> [Acts 2:42]

Jesus showed us examples of how to pray when He came to this world, many verses of the scriptures demonstrated how prayerful Jesus was. Many times He engaged in prayers alone:

> *"... now it came to pass in those days that He went to the mountain to pray, and continued all night in prayer to God."*
> [Luke 6:12]

It may be argued that because Jesus is God in man form, without prayers He would still have achieved His purpose as the Saviour of the world. But it is popularly said that we live by example and this is what Jesus has shown throughout His period on the earth. Saint Luke's gospel recorded that Jesus Christ prayed to the point that His sweat was like drops of blood:

> *"... and being in agony, He prayed more*

> *earnestly. Then His sweat became like great drops of blood falling down to the ground."*
>
> [Luke 22:44]

If Jesus could pray to this point, then as prayer warriors we need to emulate this. Jesus started with prayer and fasting in the wilderness of temptation and ended with prayer in the garden. What about you?

As virtuous women and prayer warriors we must pray until our situations change for the best that God has for us. As prayer warriors we must love prayer and be prepared to:

> *"... pray without ceasing"*
>
> [1 Thessalonians 5:17]

This is the commandment of God to us all.

Many great women in the scripture received their breakthrough as a result of their ceaseless prayers. Hannah is an example of such a woman. Hannah had been worshipping at Shiloh all her life even though she was barren. Yet, she never tired of serving God. But the faithful God who never allows His people to suffer indefinitely, eventually answered her.

> *"... and she was in bitterness of soul, and prayed to the Lord and wept in anguish. Then she made a vow."*
> [1 Samuel 1:10-11]

Hannah prayed to the Lord and He answered her with the conception and birth of Samuel, the prophet. She did not pray once and stop but continuously prayed to the Lord.

> *"... so it was year by year she went to the house of the Lord."*
> [1 Samuel 1:7]

Many benefits are lost due to a prayerless life. A virtuous woman must be prayerful and must be a dedicated person to her family and kind to others in need:

> *"... the prayer of faith will save the sick, and the Lord will raise him up, and if he has committed sins, he will be forgiven."*
>
> *[James 5:15]*

Persevering in prayer is encouraged in this scripture:

> *"You who make mention of the LORD, do not keep silent, And give Him no rest till He establishes And till He makes Jerusalem a praise in the earth."*
>
> [Isaiah 62:6-7]

Women need to be like Esther who prayed and fasted whilst petitioning God for favour with the king. According to palace protocol, no-one could have access to the king, including his wife, unless he extended his royal sceptre. But after her three days of praying and fasting, Queen Esther approached the king who extended his royal sceptre to her. She was able to overturn the death sentence over her people and bring about promotion in the palace for her uncle

Mordecai.

Prayers go a long way in showing our seriousness and urgency to God about our request. Speedy answers to prayer demand our holiness, fasting and prayer, which means a sinner can hardly receive from God if she refuses to forsake her sinful ways. God loves the sinner but hates sin; therefore if you are still living in sin, repent today so that the answers to your prayers can come forth:

> *"... the effective, fervent prayer of a righteous man[or woman] avails much."*
> *[James 5:17]*

Sometimes it is good to reach out to the poor and needy by giving the little we can to assist them; the more we do this the more we also receive mercy and favour from God. The Bible even declares that it is more rewarding to give than to receive.

> *"... the generous soul will be made rich,*

And he who waters will also be watered himself."

[Proverbs 11:25]

Chapter 6

The Power of Women

Power is an authority given to someone in order to implement or enforce discipline to accomplish a desired end. One is powerful if he has license to manipulate or oppress another but instead relents and directs power in a positive way by showing love and kindness. Power used in negative ways to fulfil a selfish end, always leads to destruction; but on the other hand, when well managed, it will bring positive results, and enable everyone to live in peace and harmony.

A woman's power in the society today is an important subject we are going to discuss under this topic. It can have a negative or positive effect on situations or circumstances depending on the one in authority. In the world today, women are in outstanding positions both in the government and private sector. We have female presidents, chancellors and prime ministers in some countries as well as in the parliaments.

Jezebel was a wife to Ahab, the king of Israel. She was not only a wife but also had so much authority over the land that she executed several prophets of God without anyone questioning why. Obadiah, the servant to king Ahab, made this known to the prophet Elijah through his report:

> *"... was it not reported to my lord what I did when Jezebel killed the prophets of the Lord, how I hid one hundred men of the Lord's prophets, fifty to a cave and fed them with bread and water?"*
>
> *[1 King 18:13]*

Jezebel was a witch and also belonged to the evil secret societies in the land. This was revealed through the request of prophet Elijah when he challenged the Baal prophets:

> *"... send and gathered all Israel to me on Mount Carmel, the four hundred and fifty prophets of Baal, and the four hundred*

> *prophets of Asherah, who eat at Jezebel's table."*
>
> [1 King 18:19]

Jezebel's abuse of power over Naboth, the owner of a vineyard, will be our case study for this topic. Jezebel's veto power in the palace made her forcefully claim Naboth's property after instructing that he be murdered. Jezebel's evil deeds made her to be the worst queen they ever had in the land

Naboth was a Jezreelite who had a vineyard next to the king's palace. King Ahab approached him with the offer to buy it, but he refused because it was an inherited property.

> *"... Naboth said to Ahab, The Lord forbid that I should give the inheritance of my fathers to you.!"*
>
> [1 King 21:3]

Naboth's response disappointed Ahab, but when he told Jezebel what had happened, she became furious and reassured him that he would have the vineyard after all.

> "... he said to her, 'because I spoke to Naboth the Jezreelite, and said to him, - Give me your vineyard for money; or else, if it pleases you, I will give you another vineyard for it. - And he answered, I will not give you my vineyard.' Then Jezebel his wife said to him, 'You now exercise authority over Israel! Arise, eat food and let your heart be cheerful; I will give you the vineyard of Naboth the Jezreelite.'"
> [1 Kings 21:6-7]

Therefore, to make sure she fulfilled her promise to her husband, she went behind her husband's back and plotted evil against Naboth. She wrote a letter in her husband's name and used his seal to convince the elders of the authenticity of the letter. She used her feminine wiles to authorise a death sentence against Naboth.

> "... she wrote letters in Ahab's name,

> *sealed them with his seal, and sent the letters to the elders and the nobles who were dwelling in the city with Naboth. She wrote saying, 'Proclaim a fast, and seat Naboth with high honour among the people and seat two men, scoundrels, before him to bear witness against him, saying, - you have blasphemed God and the king. - Then take him out and stone him that he may die.'"*
>
> [1 Kings 21:9-10]

She did not consider the motive of the king behind the possession of the vineyard. As a king, Ahab would have been in possession of many such estates. If Jezebel had been a virtuous woman, she would have advised her husband not to covet Naboth's property; but instead she encouraged him.

Think about this:

- Do you encourage your husband to fixate on evil ideas and engage in evil activities or do you discourage him?

- How do you use your power as a woman? Do you use it to change or manipulate things in your home or surroundings?

- What role do you play in delicate issues that can have a negative impact on other people's lives?

Jezebel's command was as powerful as her husband's because of her position in the community and the evil societies (cults) she belonged to. Therefore they carried out her plans as she commanded them in the letter:

> "... so the men of his city, the elders and nobles who were inhabitants of his city, did as Jezebel had said to them, as it was written in the letters which she had sent to them... Then they sent to Jezebel saying, 'Naboth has been stoned and is dead."
> [1 King 21:11 & 14]

Truly Naboth died but the sin of Jezebel and Ahab was not buried with Naboth. God eventually avenged his death on the couple:

> "'... behold I will bring calamity on you. I will take away your prosperity, and I will cut off from Ahab every male in Israel, both bond and free. I will make your house like the house of Jeroboham the son of Nabat, and like the house of Baasha the son of Ahijah, because of provocation with which you have provoke Me to anger, and made Israel sin.' And concerning Jezebel the Lord also spoke, saying 'The dogs shall eat Jezebel by the wall of Jezreel. The dogs shall eat whoever belongs to Ahab and dies in the city, and the birds of the air shall eat whoever dies in the field.'"
>
> [1 King 21:21-24]

Jezebel used her power in a negative way to accumulate wealth and fame for her husband. Now, let us examine ourselves - in what ways do we assist our husbands to be overcomers during difficult times? Jezebel murdered, defrauded and destroyed the reputation of an innocent man for her husband to achieve success. The scripture summed it up like this:

> *"... but there was no one like Ahab who sold himself to do wickedness in the sight of the Lord, because Jezebel his wife stirred him up."*
>
> [1 King 21:25]

Do you go along with your husband's plan when it is clear that he is motivated by an evil desire? If you are in Jezebel's shoes, please repent now before it is too late. Because the judgement of God was without mercy on Jezebel and Ahab, so will it be for whoever follows their example.

> *"... but he who does wrong will be repaid for what he has done, and there is no partiality."*
>
> [Colossians 3:25]

By contrast, Shiphrah and Puah were two powerful women recorded in the Bible that used their power in a positive way. These two women were the Hebrew midwives in the land of Egypt to whom King Pharaoh gave instruction to kill every male child born of the children of Israel. During the period of the Israelites' slavery in Egypt, Pharaoh noticed how they were becoming more numerous and stronger than the Egyptians.

> "... he said to his people, Look, the people
> of the children of Israel are more and
> mightier than we"
>
> [Exodus 1:9]

So, for fear they would instigate an uprising to gain their freedom, Pharoah decided that all male children of the Israelites should be put to death at birth:

> "... come let us deal shrewdly with them,
> lest they multiply, and it happen, in
> the event of war, that they also join our
> enemies and fight against us, and so go up
> out of the land."
>
> [Exodus 1:10]

These women had the power to implement Pharaoh's evil instructions to achieve his ulterior motive but they refused because they feared God:

> "... but the midwives feared God, and did not do as the king of Egypt commanded them but saved the male children alive."
> [Exodus 1:17]

The fear of God is the foundation of wisdom. Pharaoh later asked why they did not execute his instruction and they used the wisdom of God to answer the king. Because of this, God uplifted the midwives and prospered them:

> "... therefore God dealt well with the midwives, and the people multiplied and grew very mighty. And so it was, because the midwives feared God, that He provided households for them."
> [Exodus 1:20-21]

As virtuous women, we must fear God in

whatever position we hold in the society and the church of God. Watch out for the way you use the authority delegated to you by your husband in the private company of the family so that you will not sin against God. As well as the area of the gifts of God in your life, do not forget that whatever gift you have, it is from God and must be used for the glory of Him who gave it to you. Sadly, many women failed to achieve their purpose of creation through the misuse of their gift as a minister in the house of God. Many women have used their beauty to attempt to seduce ministers of God, while many have used their physical charms to destroy matrimonial homes, acquire wealth and derail the destinies of fellow brothers and sisters in Christ. Be careful how you use the power and authority given to you, and always remember to be humble:

> *"... for we brought nothing into this world, and it is certain we can carry*

nothing out."

[1 Timothy 6:7]

Chapter 7

Women of Great Faith

> "Now faith is the substance of things hoped for, the evidence of things not seen."
>
> [Hebrew 11:1]

Ironically, this statement does not make sense when it is read literally, but spiritually it is correct. It is generally understood that 'seeing is believing'; therefore to believe without seeing the substance is questionable in the eyes of men.

> "... with men it is impossible, but with God, all things are possible"
>
> [Matthew 19:26]

It is the belief of every child of God that Christ's death, resurrection, and ascension have given us hope of eternal life. Faith is the evidence of things not seen but hoped for, for every child of God. This also applies to all good things we hope for, though it has not yet come to realisation but we believe we will experience it one day.

Sarah demonstrated notable faithfulness, first to her husband and to God. Therefore, the Bible recorded her as one of the heroes of faith. She reflected what the word faith meant by hoping for the fruit of the womb even when she had passed the age of child bearing:

> "... now Abraham and Sarah were old, well advanced in age; and Sarah had passed the age of child bearing."
> [Genesis 18:11]

She was an embodiment of what faith and hope represent and how a woman can exercise her faith even when all hopes seem lost.

By contrast, Sarah's lack of faith made her laugh when God said she would conceive. [Genesis 18] Previously her lack of faith, as sarai [Genesis 16] resulted in her entreating Abram to take Hagar 'as a wife' in order to bear a child. Whilst these show a lack of faith, at some point between laughing and conceiving, her faith grew. This season of Sarah's life demonstrates that faith grows by degrees:

> *"By faith Sarah herself also received strength to conceive seed, and she bore a child when she was past the age, because she judged Him faithful who had promised."*
>
> [Hebrew 11:11]

It can encourage you to grow in faith even though your faith may seem small at the moment. I would encourage you not to give up on what you have heard from God. Keep believing and one day it will happen.:

> *"... so shall My word be that goes forth from My mouth; it shall not return to Me void, but it shall accomplish what I please, and it shall prosper in the thing for which I sent it."*
>
> [Isaiah 55:11]

No matter the circumstances of our lives or families, we must always believe in Jesus Christ who can do all things, and by His mighty power, bring hope into our hopeless situations. Do not forget that Sarah drew her strength from God when she needed it to accomplish what God had purposed for her life. On this occasion, the Bible counted this woman as an hero of faith because of her ability to draw and utilise the strength from the Originator of faith. God is looking for women who will rely totally on His power to do the impossible.

Faithful women will wait upon the Lord in their prayers and fasting to attack and win battles both within and outside their homes. They are women who are ready to impress Jesus by their faith like the woman with the issue of blood who believed that by touching the helm of His garment, she would receive her healing and it was so. They are women who, despite the fact that they spent all they have on physicians or other human resources, are still willing to touch Jesus by their faith. The scriptures record that the woman with the issue of blood:

> *"… had suffered many things from many physicians. She had spent all that she had and was no better, but rather grew worse.*
> *When she heard about Jesus she came behind Him in the crowd and touched His garment. For she said, if only I may touch His clothes, I shall be made well."*
> [Mark 5:26-28]

Truly the faith of the woman made her well and ended all her sufferings and divine restoration followed her healing. Jesus said to her:

> *"daughter your faith has made you well go in peace and be healed of your affliction."*
> [Mark 5:34]

I believe that this is a message of God to you as you are reading this chapter. Jesus Christ is the great Physician who is ready to heal you and set you free from all your afflictions if you will only have that faith in Him. Believe that He is the only One who can do what man cannot do and you shall be healed.

Ruth was an example of a virtuous woman who was faithful to her mother-in-law even after the death of her husband.

> *"And she said, 'look your sister in-law has gone back to her people and to her gods; return after your sister in-law.' but Ruth said, 'entreat me not to leave you, or turn back from following after you; For wherever you go, I will go; and wherever you lodge, I will lodge; your people shall be my people, and your God, my God.'"*
> [Ruth 1:15-16]

A *v*irtuous woman like Ruth is a prime example of one whose worth is far above rubies, she is the type that the heart of her husband will safely trust.

> *"... who can find a virtuous wife? For her worth is far above rubies. The heart of her husband safely trusts her."*
>
> [Proverbs 31:10-11]

Ruth decided to follow her mother in-law without hesitation and with total commitment to her God and people. Spiritually, this is pointing out what is expected of a virtuous woman. She must commit her life totally to God, and take the decision of lifetime to serve God and not other gods. Other gods may come in the form of clothing, hairstyles, jewellery, and forgetting what the scriptures says about moderations in all things.

> *"... in like manner also, that the women adorn themselves in modest apparel, with propriety and moderation, not with braided hair or gold or pearls or costly clothing."*
>
> [1 Timothy 2:9]

Please do not misunderstand me here! It

is good to look good and even God wants His children to put on their best because we are not serving a wretched God, but a God of prosperity who is abundantly able to prosper us. But whenever a child of God borrows money to buy or acquire clothing, jewellery, shoes and other outward adornments because she wants to be fashionable or look better off, then she has exceeded the boundaries of moderation and began to serve other gods.

Other gods to avoid include hedonism, feminism - playing the role of a man or husband, lesbianism, drunkenness, fornication, adultery, witchcraft and occultism.

> *"Changing the glory of the incorruptible God to an image made like corruptible man– and birds and four footed animals and creeping things. Therefore God also gave them up to uncleanness, in the lust of their hearts, to dishonour their bodies among themselves, who exchange the*

> *truth of God for the lie and worshipped and served the creature rather than the Creator, who is blessed forever, Amen. For this reason God gave them up to vile passion. For even their women exchange the natural use for what is against nature ... "*
>
> [Roman 1:23-27]

If you fall into any of these categories, please repent today and turn to God.

As a virtuous woman, you must be faithful to your husband, love and cherish him. No matter what he has done in the past or present, your love for him must endure. You must strive to bring joy and laughter to him, and so delight in you. As a virtuous woman, you must be able to manage your home without comparing your husband with others as this will not make things go smoothly at home. Be aware that men do not always appreciate comparison when it comes to personality and ability with the affairs at home. They love women who appreciate their little efforts and praise them even when they do not deserve it. We must be women who fear God in all our dealings, and be of few words because in many words one stumbles.

> *"... for in the multitude of dreams and many words there is also vanity, but fear God."*
>
> [Ecclesiastes 5:7]

Always use spiritual eyes to see things rather than natural physical sight because how far we will go in life is determined by how much we see in the spirit. If we look just beyond, then we shall not move far but if we see greater things that God has prepared for us, then our achievement will be without measure. This cannot be possible without faith because it is our faith that God will capitalise on for our breakthrough. Do not forget that there is a wilderness before Canaan; therefore, before we can get to the promised land we need to apply faith and endurance which will see us through rough times.

> *"... for without faith it is impossible to please Him, for he who comes to God must believe that He is, and that He is a rewarder of those who diligently seek Him."*
>
> [Hebrews 11:6]

Let us all bear in mind that what we see here in the world is temporary but the kingdom of God we hope for is everlasting.

> *"While we do not look at the things which are seen, but at the things which are not seen, for the things which are seen are temporary, but the things which are not seen are eternal."*
>
> [2 Corinthians 4:18]

Chapter 8

Women as Vehicles of Restoration

"... and she will bring forth a Son, and you shall call His name Jesus, for He will save His people from their sins."

[Matthew 1:21]

The vehicle in the real sense serves the purpose of transportation, conveyancing and the movement of living and non living things from one place to another. In this chapter, I am using the comparison of women to vehicles as a metaphor. Mary was the vehicle through which Jesus Christ came into this world. The first generation of mankind sinned through the serpent's deception of Eve in the garden of Eden.

"... when the woman saw that the tree was good for food, and that it was pleasant to the eyes, and a tree to be desired to make one wise, she took of the fruit thereof, and did eat, and gave also unto her husband

> *with her; and he did eat."*
>
> *[Genesis 3:6]*

Therefore although a woman caused the downfall at the beginning, ironically God used a woman to restore the situation. Eve played a vital role in the garden of Eden to bring sin to mankind and God chose Mary through whom to conceive and gave birth to Jesus Christ who was destined to bring forgiveness of sin to mankind:

> *"... but while he thought about these things, behold, an angel of the Lord appeared to him in a dream, saying, 'Joseph, son of David, do not be afraid to take to you Mary your wife, for that which is conceived in her is of the Holy Spirit, and she will bring forth a Son, and you shall call His name Jesus, for He will save His people from their sins'"*
>
> [Matthew 1:20-21]

Mary, the virgin, was the instrument for the purpose of restoration. Her virginity was just one of the characteristics that God found fit which gave her the privilege to become the vehicle that brought Jesus Christ to the world.

> *"... and having come in, the angel said to her, 'Rejoice, highly favoured one, the Lord is with you; blessed are you among women!'"*
>
> [Luke 1:28]

The purpose of Jesus is to bridge the broken relationship between man and God which was caused by the disobedient act of Adam and Eve. Although Mary was by no means sinless, God chose Mary, in part because she was a virgin, which symbolises one without spot, one who has the ability to withstand dirt, light that darkness cannot overcome, an outstanding person who does not care about the comment of the public so far it is God's will, a virtuous woman who does not care about the affairs of this world but heaven. Mary was highly moral and spotless when it came to purity.

Women have always being known as world changers and record breakers where restoration is concerned. Woman like Esther restored peace to the Jews of her time. Haman plotted death because of the hatred he had for just one Jew, Mordecai, and he wanted to engage in the murder of all the Jews. Queen Esther's intervention silenced the death sentence hanging over the land. Women tend to possess the calmness and perseverance necessary to see problems through to resolution. They embrace the attitude of - 'I won't give up till I see it done!' This helped in the recovery of Naman, the captain of the army of Syria, from his leprosy by virtue of the slave maiden's determination to be of help.

The question is - are you prepared to put to work the qualities which God has deposited in you to achieve His divine purposes? Will He be pleased with you, as He was with Mary? Think about this because in this present age God is looking for outstanding women who will be the vehicles to restore the damaged world, the wounded souls and lost sheep. Jesus is relying on you to bridge the gap between Him and your loved ones and to bring back to God the backsliders in your community. Make a quick assessment of your spiritual life with reference to the highlighted qualities of Mary, the virgin. Do you think that you will qualify to be a vehicle to restore sinners back to God if you do not amend your ways today?

Chapter 9

Victorious Women

A virtuous woman is victorious; she can be a worthy example for other people to emulate. Deborah is such an example; she is recorded in the Bible as a prophetess, a judge and an outstanding warrior of God who brought victory to the children of Israel.

> *"Deborah, a prophetess, the wife of Lapidoth, she judged Israel at that time. And she dwelt under the palm tree of Deborah between Ramah and Bethel in mount Ephraim: and the children of Israel came up to her for judgment."*
>
> [Judges 4:4-5]

She challenged the power and the authority of Barak, who bowed to her:

> *"... she sent and called Barak the son of Abinoam out of Kedesh-naphtali, and said unto him, 'Hath not the LORD God of Israel commanded, saying, Go and draw toward mount Tabor, and take with*

thee ten thousand men of the children of Naphtali and of the children of Zebulun? And I will draw unto thee to the river Kishon, Sisera, the captain of Jabin's army, with his chariots and his multitude; and I will deliver him into thine hand.' And Barak said unto her, 'If thou wilt go with me, then I will go: but if thou wilt not go with me, then I will not go.' and she said, 'I will surely go with thee: notwithstanding the journey that thou takest shall not be for thine honour; for the Lord shall sell Sisera into the hand of a woman.' And Deborah arose, and went with Barak to Kedesh."

[Judges 4:6-8 KJV]

God gave the Israelites victory over Sisera through a woman. Please take note that although Deborah led the battle, this does not change the plan of God for men to play the role as the head of the family. Although you may be a prayer warrior or leader in your church or hold any other leadership post, this does not place you over your husband. We later read in the scripture that Barak took up his position as the head at the frontline when he emerged at the tail end of the battle.

> "... the Lord discomfited Sisera, and all his chariots, and all his host, with the edge of the sword before Barak; so that Sisera lighted down off his chariot, and fled away on his feet."
>
> [Judges 4:15]

As a victorious woman, you must be the key that opens the door to victorious testimonies from the battlefield of life on a daily basis. The world is a battlefield full of different challenges and whoever survives is the winner. As a victorious woman, it is your responsibility to train your children how to fight in the battlefield of life and especially how to overcome challenges. There have been a lot of casualties and many wounded soldiers because some women did not train their children how to handle the situations of life. The questions that always come to my mind in the case of the unspeakable attitude of the sons of Eli in their society is; 'where was their mother?' or 'have they no mother?' It could be argued that Eli was there but the role of mother and father are different in the upbringing of the children.

> *"He who spares his rod hates his son, but he who loves him disciplines him promptly."*
> [Proverbs 13:24]

Whether we like it or not, mothers indirectly control the affairs of the children in the house. Because of the fact that the child stays in her womb for nine months, there is often a closer bond with her than with the father. Furthermore, mothers usually spend more time with their children in the house. While some mothers train their children, they may not have started early enough to give full training and half training is more or less no training. Most importantly, the mother in the house must be a role model bearing in mind that the children will follow her example.

In the church or community, you must be ready to stand up as a solution to the wrongs in the society, and act as medication for the sick in your community. There have been incidences such as stabbings, gun crime, kidnapping, and gang culture to mention a few. Women in the community must not overlook these opportunities to rise up and work together by organising prayer meetings on how to deal with the situation in every home. No one will argue that the root of all evils in the society are to be found in the home. When the home is at peace, there will be peace in the church and in the community. As victorious warriors of the Mighty God, your battles must be won in your home, church (through intercessory prayer and fasting) and even in the community.

A victorious woman must always aim at winning the ultimate battle against the devil by living a holy life. Live what you are teaching your children. 'Do as I do' is the best way to impart knowledge and morals in the children. Your life is your message to your children and people around you. Living by example may cause you to lose friends who encourage bad habits in your life; but such habits will not help your children to live a godly life. Paul states:

> *"... all things are lawful for me, but not all things are helpful; all things are lawful for me, but not all things edify."*
> [1 Corinthians 10:23]

Achieving the ultimate goal which is to inherit the kingdom of God, is the heavenly expectation of a virtuous woman. Ask yourself - am I a victorious woman? If not, amend your ways today and turn to Jesus while you still have the opportunity.

Chapter 10

Devoted Women

Women who stay focused will be able to move mountains. She devotes her 'all' in working things out. Staying positive in spite of negative circumstances, and carrying on when it seems there are no more options are some of the qualities of a devoted woman. Ruth said to Naomi:

> *"Entreat me not to leave you, or to turn back from following after you; for wherever you go, I will go; and wherever you lodge, I will lodge; your people shall be my people, and your God, my God. Where you die, I will die, and there will I be buried. The Lord do so to me, and more also, if anything but death parts you and me."*
> [Ruth 1:16-17 KJV]

When Naomi saw the determination of Ruth to go with her, she stopped trying to convince her to leave, and started sharing her plans with her.

When you are a determined woman, God will share His plans with you. Wayward children need devoted parents who will change their lives.

> *"I appeal to you for my son, Onesimus, whom I have begotten while in my chains,who once was unprofitable to you, but now is profitable to you and to me."*
> [Philemon 1:10-11]

In the above verse, Paul as a spiritual father, explains that even a wayward and profitless child can change and become profitable to the parents and society.

An adage says - 'Behind any successful man there is always a woman.' For the purpose of the study, I will re-structure the phrase as follows - 'Behind every successful man there is always a devoted woman.' It is a devoted woman, in both physical and spiritual matters, who can make a home as well as assist her husband to achieve his goals in life. It is not because of what she is academically or her status in the society, but her fulfilment of God's plan and purpose as a *"helper fit"* for her husband. The Bible gives this quality to summarise such a woman [Proverbs 31:14-18]

Female devotion is hard to find in today's society. Many women have taken the view that 'if it doesn't work, I'm leaving.' Many women are changing men as often as they change their clothes, and remarry so many times, ending each marriage with the same excuse as the previous one. Women, do you know that the only excuse for divorce in God's eyes, is sexual immorality? [Matthew 19:9]

Many women now compete with men in many ways just to avoid their responsibilities as a devoted helper in their families. They are not ready to look after their families but prefer to travel around the world. They are not willing to support their husband to achieve his goals in life but rather jump in and out of marriage. Many others prefer to remain as single mothers for life because they are not ready to take on board the role of wife. This is one of the reasons we have a lot of crime on our streets today. Are you among this group? If yes, you need to go before God in prayers to break the curse.

The Bible describes the roles of a devoted woman and gives a lot of examples of such women. An example of this was the mother of Moses who sacrificed her motherhood to look after her son whom the daughter of Pharaoh had taken home from the river. You may ask why was he in the river? He was there because his mother wanted to protect him from the death sentence passed on to every male child of Israel:

> *"... and Pharaoh's daughter said to her, 'Go.' And the maid went and called the child's mother. And Pharaoh's daughter said unto her, take this child away, and nurse it for me, and I will give thee thy wages. And the woman took the child, and nursed it. And the child grew, and*

she brought him unto Pharaoh's daughter, and he became her son. And she called his name Moses and she said, 'because I drew him out of the water.'"

[Exodus 2:7-9]

When Jesus was crucified, he handed over his beloved disciple to his mother, and his mother to him. Jesus cared so much about his mother that he wanted to ensure she would be well looked after in his physical absence. [John 19:26-27] Whom do you leave your children with when you go to work? Who looks after your husband during your business trips? Sadly, many women have lost their homes, children and families due to such neglect. A devoted woman sees the welfare of her home as a package and never leaves any stone unturned.

If you are a mother reading this book and you are separated from your husband and children for no good reason other than your own selfish desires, you are causing your children to suffer; because there is no way their father can fill the vacuum of the love and touch of a mother. Even if another woman comes in as a new wife, she cannot look after your children as you will do. Therefore, repent quickly and make things right as soon as you can. Moses grew up and became a prophet of God through whom the whole house of Israel was delivered from Egyptian bondage. You never know what God has purposed for your children so throw away your pride and go back to your husband and do your best to make it work. Surely God will honour your decision.

Chapter 11

Women's Position as Mothers

The woman's position at home as a mother is a vital role; to deprive her children of such would be a great loss. The role of a mother is an essential part of the child's life, growth and development, not only in physical but spiritual matters. Children want to be loved and cared for and when this is lacking, emotionally they are ruined for life; such children tend to grow up to be truants, aggressors and vandals.

There is a story of two women during the reign of king Solomon in Israel. Both mothers slept at night with their babies by their sides. Unfortunately one of the babies died overnight and the mother of the dead baby swapped the baby with the living. In the morning, the case was taken to the king who proposed that he cut the living baby into two to give half to each woman. The true mother intervened because of her love for her child.

> *"Then the woman whose son was living spoke to the king, for she yearned with compassion for her son; and she said: 'O my lord, give her the living child, and by no means kill him!' But the other said, 'Let him be neither mine nor yours, but divide him.'"*
>
> [1 Kings 3:26 KJV]

It is speculated that the absence of their mother in the life of the daughters of Lot may have caused them to plot to sleep with their drunken father in order to conceive offspring. [Genesis 19:30-38]

Similarly the unruly attitude of Ham, the son of Noah, could possibly have been a result of the lack of a mother's guidance because the Bible doesn't mention the presence of their mother. [Genesis 9:22]

In what ways are you not fulfilling your role as a mother? Perhaps you are a single mother. There have been many great single mothers who have single handedly trained and educated their children to university level and most of these children have made progress in life. In the scripture we have seen Rahab the harlot who saved her entire family from Jericho's destruction. [Joshua 6:23]

Another example is the widow of Zarephath and her son who were made rich by giving Elijah the only food they had left to live [1 Kings 17:9-10]

There are many model mothers referred to in the scripture; among them is the mother of the two sons of Zebedee who asked Jesus that her sons might sit at His side in the Kingdom:

> *"Then the mother of Zebedee's sons came to Him with her sons kneeling down and asking something from Him. And He said to her, 'what do you wish?' She said to Him,'Grant that these two sons of mine may sit, one on Your right hand and the other on the left, in Your kingdom'"*
> [Matthew 20:20-21]

Many parents today, do not care about the salvation of their children as the mother of the sons of Zebedee. All they care about is their business, career and pleasure, forgetting the fact that the children are their tomorrow. The Bible instructs:

> *"Train up a child in the way he should go: and when he is old, he will not depart from it."*
>
> [Proverbs 22:6]

When you train your children in the way they should go, they will not go astray. In what ways are you training your child? Or is your child your boss at home as is often the case. In the UK children are regarded by law as adults at the age of 16 years. If Jesus stayed under his parents' roof till the age of 30, before He commenced His ministry, you need to fulfil your role ensuring your children receive a full training before leaving home. Do not forget that the scripture says:

> *"Do not withhold correction from a child,*

For if you beat him with a rod, he will not die. You shall beat him with a rod, and deliver his soul from hell"
[Proverbs 23:13-14]

The rod to a grown up child or young adult may be implemented by word of mouth rather than a physical rod. That reminds me of what happened to me when I was a young adult under my parents' roof; my father corrected me with strong language regarding a simple mistake. It was not easy to accept at the time but it straightened me out and even till now has become part of my life's pattern.

Here are some tips on how to train your child as a Christian:

"Lo, children are an heritage of the Lord"
[Psalm:127:3 KJV]

God loves children and He is always angry when they are mistreated yet He has an interest in their dignity and integrity.

It is important that you must be a good role model at home - not a quarrelsome, lying or dubious parent or mother.

The family that prays together stays together. Learn to pray together as a family and let your children know the importance of praying together.

Do not give them too much freedom that will make them grow up to be lawless individuals in the society.

In training children, you must know how to be patient and endure. Do not rebuke your child in anger and do not be provoked to the point of swearing or cursing your child because *"the power of life and death is in the tongue"*. [Proverbs 18:21]

Show that you love and care for them at all times, so that they can grow to love others. Lack of this has caused many mothers to lose their children.

Show them that you appreciate them. Many of the children on the street today feel unwanted, insecure and unloved by their parents. This is why they prefer to stay on the street than at home.

Monitor their growth and lead them through the stages of maturity such as puberty and menstruation.

Apply the principle of confidentiality in dealing with their sexual and personal matters in order to enhance trust between parent and children.

Make yourself available in order to enable them to open up to you from the depth of their minds and share their secrets.

If your child open up to you about their thoughts and if their desire is contrary to the word of God, you must not attack them but rather in love correct and redirect their desire in line with the word of God.

Let the Word of God be their daily directory and dictionary of life. Let them be firmly rooted in the Word.

> *"How can a young man cleanse his way?*
> *By taking heed according to Your word."*
> [Psalm 119:9]

In a nutshell, parents need the wisdom of God in the upbringing of their children. Therefore pray for it and believe that God will grant you His divine wisdom in doing this.

> *"Through wisdom a house is built, And*
> *by understanding it is established."*
> [Proverbs 24:3]

Chapter 12

Women's Position in the House of God

Women have played and will continue to play major roles of stewardship in the body of Christ because of their potential to turn and change situations around for good.

For example, the seven daughters of Zelophehad raised with Moses the issue of their father's inheritance in the absence of a son. Moses consulted God who decreed that in the absence of a son, a man's inheritance would pass to his daughters. [Numbers 27:1-8] Thus a man's inheritance - his land - was not lost if he died without a son.

Women's influence in the early church history cannot be under-estimated. Martha was the communicator with Jesus. [John 11:20-24]

In the upper room, the Holy Spirit fell on all who gathered together, which included women.

> *"Then they returned to Jerusalem from the mount called Olivet, which is near Jerusalem, a Sabbath day's journey. And when they had entered, they went up into the upper room where they were staying: Peter, James, John, and Andrew; Philip and Thomas; Bartholomew and Matthew; James the son of Alphaeus and Simon the Zealot; and Judas the son of James. These all continued with one accord in prayer and supplication, with the women and Mary the mother of Jesus, and with His brothers"*
>
> [Acts 1:12-14]

The position and role of women in the house of God caused a lot of controversy in the early church. Apostle Paul instructed:

> *"Let your women keep silent in the churches, for they are not permitted to speak; but they are to be submissive, as the law also says."*
>
> [1 Corinthians 14:34]

This had caused a great argument within the congregation. Why? Because the women in the church wanted to take over the affairs in the church and have the same rights as men. According to Jewish law, women were not recognised on an equal footing with men in the society. For example, in the synagogue the women always sit separately from men and during the census, they only count men and not women and their children. [Exodus 30:12, Numbers 1:2]

Paul therefore emphasised the law of Moses, because they feared the penalty attached to law, and moreover in order to caution women from committing the same error that happened in the garden of Eden. It could also be in order to obey the custom of the Jews, not to register individual women as citizen but to acknowledge them through their husbands. Apostle Paul also gave the same advice:

"Let a woman learn in silence with all submission and I do not permit a woman

> *to teach or to have authority over a man, but to be in silence. For Adam was formed first then Eve."*
>
> [1 Timothy 2:12-14]

Does it mean that a woman must not talk or ask questions in the church when necessary? No, but for the purpose of godliness and to secure orderliness during the crisis in the church of God in Corinth. He further cautioned:

> *"So that you may know how you ought to conduct yourself in the house of God, which is the pillar and ground of the truth, and without controversy great is the mystery of godliness."*
>
> [1 Timothy 3:15-16]

Keeping silence in the church is not the standard of God when it comes to the work of God. The Bible states:

> *"... for the gifts and calling of God are*

irrevocable"

[Roman 11:29]

Whether you are a woman or man, you are called into the vineyard of God as workers for a divine harvest. In the Old Testament we read about five women who were prophetesses:

> "**Miriam the prophetess**, *the sister of Aaron, took a timbrel in her hand; and all the women went out after her with timbrels and with dances."* [Exodus 15:20]

> "**Deborah, a prophetess**, *the wife of Lapidoth, she judged Israel at that time."* [Judges 4:4]

> *"So Hilkiah the priest, and Ahikam, and Achbor, and Shaphan, and Asahiah, went unto* **Huldah the prophetess,** *the wife of Shallum the son of Tikvah, the son of Harhas, keeper of the wardrobe; (now she dwelt in Jerusalem in the second quarter;) and they communed with her."* [2 Kings 22:14]

> "My God, think thou upon Tobiah and Sanballat according to these their works, and on **the prophetess Noadiah,** and the rest of the prophets, that would have put me in fear."
> [Nehemiah 6:14]

> "I went **unto the prophetess;** (wife of prophet Isaiah) and she conceived, and bare a son. Then said the LORD to me, Call his name Maher-shalal-hash-baz." [Isaiah 8:3]

These are but a few out of the many women who had the call of God upon the.

The story changed in the New Testament where we see a tremendous movement of women's ministries. The Samarian woman at the well became the first lady evangelist because the Bible records that people accepted Jesus because of her testimony.

> "Come and see a Man who told me all things that I ever did. Could this be the Christ? Ten went out of the city and came to Him...and many Samaritans of that city

*believed in Him **because of the word of the woman** who testified, "He told me all that I ever did."*

[John 4:29-30,39]

Women were the first to witness the resurrection of Jesus Christ:

"Jesus said to her, 'woman why are you weeping? Whom are you seeking?' She, supposed Him to be the gardener, said to Him, 'Sir if have carried Him away, tell me where you have laid Him, and I will take Him away.' Jesus said to her, 'Mary!' she turned and said to Him 'Rabboni!'"

[John 20:15-16]

Dorcas was another woman in the scripture who had zeal for the welfare of the widows; even when she died, the women rallied around and called for Apostle Peter who brought her back to life.

There was a lady pastor called Priscilla who

worked alongside her husband Aquila in ministry. Therefore, women are not meant to keep silent in the house of God but to serve in His vineyard with all humility.

Chapter 13

Women's Position in the Community

Women in the Old Testament played notable roles in the community. Women have always been in support of peace, progress and harmony in society.

For example, the midwives Shiphuah and Puah in Egypt, did all in their power to fulfil the will of God to keep the male offspring alive during and following child birth.

Women have always played a large part in giving and sowing. During the offering of the tabernacle, women were part of the success:

> "... all the women who were gifted artisans spun yarn with their hands, and brought what they had spun, of blue, purple, and scarlet, and fine linen. And all the women whose hearts stirred with wisdom spun yarn of goats' hair."
> [Numbers 35:25-26]

Women of the scriptures were at the forefront in battles whether they played both passive and active roles. It was recorded that a wise woman saved a city which Joab wanted to destroy. By her wisdom she negotiated with Joab the captain of the army of Israel; and by wisdom rallied a town cry for deliverance and eventually succeeded in wining the people's heart and delivered the head of the wanted man to Joab:

> "'I am among the peaceable and faithful in Israel. You seek to destroy a city and a mother in Israel. Why would you swallow up the inheritance of the LORD?' and Joab answered and said, 'Far be it, far be it from me, that I should swallow up or destroy! that is not so. But a man from the mountains of Ephraim, Sheba the son of Bichri by name, has raised his hand against the king, against David. Deliver him only, and I will depart from the city.'
>
> So the woman said to Joab, 'Watch, his head will be thrown to you over the wall.'

> *Then the woman in her wisdom went to all the people. And they cut off the head of Sheba the son of Bichri, and threw it out to Joab. Then he blew a trumpet, and they withdrew from the city, every man to his tent. So Joab returned to the king at Jerusalem."*
>
> [2 Samuel 20:18-21]

In the New Testament, Mary Magdalene anointed Jesus' feet and Judas, one of the disciples, rebuked her but Jesus said:

> *"Why did you trouble the woman? For she has done a good work for Me... assuredly, I say to you, wherever this gospel is preached in the whole world, what this woman has done will also be told as a memorial to her."*
>
> [Matthew 26:10-13]

On many occasions, Jesus Christ addressed the multitude which means men, women and children. Women were among the disciples of Jesus as it was recorded in the book of Acts, notably in the upper room after His ascension.

Women today can also play vital roles to make it worth while to live in our communities. For ages women have been hiding behind men, and claiming to be the weaker vessels. If God can use Esther to deliver her community through fasting and prayer, then He can use you too - *"Yes, YOU!!!"*

The impact of virtuous women in our dispensation can never be under estimated. This generation has seen women who are queens, presidents, prime ministers and members of parliaments to mention but a few. You too can pray for something good to happen in this nation and the world as a whole, and for God to equip women for His purposes. If a woman like Deborah can fight and prevail, then you can also be a warrior for Christ.

What does it take to influence your

community?

>Love God, the Father of all.

>Love your neighbour as yourself and love the unlovable.

>Find out who you are and your purpose on earth.

>Write your vision and make it plain.

>Plan and research for the resources you will need to fulfil your vision.

>Determine to make your own impact.

>Be ready to sacrifice and give your all.

>Make up your mind to work hard.

Chapter 14

Keys to becoming a Virtuous Woman

A Woman's nature from generations past is to be un-submissive. This is why Eve took it upon herself to deal with the serpent on her own even though her husband was with her and acted passively. Becoming a godly woman is the only way to make the difference in the society and at home. It is therefore important to cast out this nature and take up the new nature of humbleness in order to enjoy your husband, family and Jesus Christ:

> *"If indeed you have heard Him and have been taught by Him as the truth is in Jesus that you put off, concerning your former conduct, the old man to the deceitful lusts, and be renewed in the spirit of your mind and that you put on the new man which created according to God, in the righteousness and holiness."*
> [Ephesians 4:21-24]

Allow the Holy Spirit to direct and guide your home and do not forget that *"... love covers a lot of sins"* and *"... love is not proud, does not parade itself"* [1 Corinthians 13] Submit totally to your husband in love and according to the will of God. Love is the greatest key that opens the door to becoming a virtuous woman.

Keys to Success

Faithfulness to your husband and household. *"For by means of a whorish woman, a man is brought to a piece of bread: and the adulteress will hunt for the precious life."* [Proverbs 6:26]

Co-operate with your husband just as Sarah did with Abraham when they entertained the angels on an errand to Sodom. *"So Abraham hurried into the tent to Sarah and said, "Quickly, make ready three measures of fine meal; knead it and make cakes. Abraham ran to the herd, took a tender and good calf, gave it to a* young man, and he hastened to prepare it" [Genesis 18:6-7]

Total Submission to your husband only in the Lord, meaning if your husband want to force you do contrary to God's Word, then you must go unto your knees to pray against his instruction.

"Wives, likewise be submissive to your husbands, that even if some do not obey the word, they - without a word, may be won by the conduct of their wives."
[1 Peter 3:1]

Communication must not be lacking but it must be at the right time. This requires the wisdom of God and the direction of the Holy Spirit to know the right time.

"Do not let your mouth cause your flesh to sin, nor say before the messenger of God that it was an error. Why should God be angry at your excuse and destroy the work of your hands? For in the multitude

of dreams and many words there is also vanity. But fear God."
[Ecclesiastes 5:6-7]

Love must be without hypocrisy and it must be absolute within the family.

"Husbands (wives) ought to love their own wives (husbands) as their own bodies; he (she) who loves his wife (her husband) loves himself (herself). For no one ever hates his own flesh, but nourishes and cherishes it, just as the Lord does the church."
[Ephesians 5:28-29]

This Scripture can be appropriated to wives because husbands and wives are one flesh in God's eyes.

Allow the Holy Spirit to rule and direct the affairs of your home. *"For as many as are led by the Spirit of God are the children of God."* [Roman 8:14]

If you are not born again, please humble yourself and call Jesus Christ into your life, for without Him there cannot be deliverance from the hand of Satan. He is the only way to Salvation, and is coming back to take those who believe in Him to be with Him for eternity. This is the greatest achievement anyone can hope for:

"Let us be glad and rejoice and give Him glory, for the marriage of the Lamb has come, and His wife has made herself ready and to her it was granted to be arrayed in the fine linen, clean and bright, for the fine linen is the righteous acts of the saints."

[Revelation 19:7-8]

A virtuous woman must be a woman of outstanding personality, a woman of integrity, unequal and remarkable personality in the community. Solomon in the book of Proverbs states that:

> "A gracious woman retains honour."
>
> [Proverbs 11:16]

These are some of the characteristics of an outstanding woman according to the scriptures:

She acknowledges God as the source of her strength, believing that she can only do all things through Him:

> "For every house is built by someone, but He who builds all things is God."
>
> [Hebrews 3:4]

Her behaviour is worthy of emulation:

> "... the older women likewise that they be reverent in behaviour, not slanderers, not given to much wine, teachers of good things that they admonish the young women to love their husbands, to love their children."
>
> [Titus 2:3-4]

She is willing and ready to train her children

in the ways of the Lord:

> *"Train up a child in the way he should go: and when he is old, he will not depart from it."*
> [Proverbs 22:6]

She works hard:

> *"She girdeth her loins with strength, and strengtheneth her arms. She perceiveth that her merchandise is good: her candle goeth not out by night. She layeth her hands to the spindle, and her hands hold the distaff."*
> [Proverbs 31:17-19]

She has the mind of a sage:

> *"She openeth her mouth with wisdom; and in her tongue is the law of kindness."*
> [Proverbs 31:26]

She makes her husband proud:

> *"She maketh herself coverings of tapestry;*

> her clothing is silk and purple. Her
> husband is known in the gates, when he
> sitteth among the elders of the land."
>
> [Proverbs 31:22-23]

She is trustworthy:

> "The heart of her husband doth safely
> trust in her, so that he shall have no need
> of spoil."
>
> [Proverbs 31:11]

Sees to the welfare of others:

> "She stretcheth out her hand to the poor;
> yea, she reacheth forth her hands to the
> needy."
>
> [Proverbs 31:20]

She bridles her tongue:

> "For the lips of a strange woman drop
> as an honeycomb, and her mouth is
> smoother than oil. But her end is bitter as
> wormwood, sharp as a two-edged sword.
> Her feet go down to death; her steps take

hold on hell."

[Proverbs 5:3-5]

She is a peaceful woman:

"It is better to dwell in the wilderness, than with a contentious and an angry woman."

[Proverbs 21:19]

She is a good ambassador for Christ and her household:

"Her children arise up, and call her blessed; her husband also, and he praiseth her. Many daughters have done virtuously, but thou excellest them all."

[Proverbs 31:28-29]

She is God-fearing:

"Favour is deceitful, and beauty is vain: but a woman that feareth the LORD, she shall be praised."

[Proverbs 31:30]

Appendix

Women's Customs, Culture and Fashion

The Old Testament moreso than the New elaborated on the custom, culture and tradition of women in the community of the children of Israel. The law and custom, culture and tradition of the Israelites are interwoven. We know that they have customs of marriage. For example, when Abraham sent his servant to his father's house to look for a wife for Isaac:

> *"Abraham said unto his eldest servant of his house, that ruled over all that he had, 'Put, I pray thee, thy hand under my thigh and I will make thee swear by the LORD, the God of heaven, and the God of the earth, that thou shalt not take a wife unto my son of the daughters of the Canaanites, among whom I dwell. But thou shalt go unto my country, and to my kindred, and take a wife unto my son*

> Isaac.'"
>
> [Genesis 24:2-4 KJV]

The same procedure took place when it was time for Jacob to get married; this time it was a woman from the mother's brother he was told to marry:

> *"Isaac called Jacob, and blessed him, and charged him, and said unto him, 'Thou shalt not take a wife of the daughters of Canaan. Arise, go to Padan-aram, to the house of Bethuel thy mother's father; and take thee a wife from thence of the daughters of Laban thy mother's brother.'"*
>
> [Genesis 28:1-2 KJV]

In the scripture, there is no formal marriage ceremony. Once it was confirmed and agreements were reached, the woman automatically became the wife, though there was also a 'betrothal period' before marriage such as between Mary and Joseph and between us and Christ.

Presents were taken by the servant of Abraham to give to the family of Rebecca, but these were not a formal dowry:

> *"The **servant** took ten camels of the camels of his master, and departed; for all the goods of his master were in his hand: and he arose, and went to Mesopotamia, unto the city of Nahor."*
> [Genesis 24:10]

> *"... it came to pass, that, when **Abraham's servant** heard their words, he worshipped the LORD, bowing himself to the earth and the servant brought forth jewels of silver, and jewels of gold, and raiment, and gave them to Rebekah: he gave also to her brother and to her mother precious things."*
> [Genesis 24:52-53]

In Exodus we read of a bride-price, a shadow of that which Christ has paid for us:

> *"If a man entices a virgin who is not*

> *betrothed, and lies with her, he shall surely pay the bride-price for her to be his wife. If her father utterly refuses to give her to him, he shall pay money according to the bride-price of virgins.*
>
> [Exodus 22:16-17]

The mode of dressing in the scripture is nothing compared to what it is now fashionable. There is nothing new under the heavens, for example the use of nose rings has been in existence since the time of Abraham. It was used on Rebecca as a proposal for wedlock between her and Isaac:

> *"'I asked her', and said,' Whose daughter art thou'? and she said, 'the daughter of Bethuel, Nahor's son, whom Milcah bare unto him': and I put the earring upon her face, (nose) and the bracelets upon her hands."*
>
> [Genesis 24:47 KJV]

Several places in the scriptures point to the use of earrings and bracelets. The misuse of them brought punishment on the users:

> "Moses returned unto the Lord, and said, 'Oh, this people have sinned a great sin, and have made them **gods of gold.** Yet now, if thou wilt forgive their sin…and if not, blot me, I pray thee, out of thy book which thou hast written' and the Lord said; unto Moses, 'Whosoever hath sinned against me, him will I blot out of my book. Therefore now go, lead the people unto the place of which I have spoken unto thee: behold, mine Angel shall go before thee: nevertheless in the day when I visit I will visit their sin upon them.' And the Lord plagued the people, because they made the calf, which Aaron made."
>
> [Exodus 32:31-34]

As a Christian, it is not an absolute rule that a woman must not wear earrings but the Bible recommends moderation and modesty. Whatever you wear that you think could make another think of committing sin, is to deviate from moderation and this becomes a sin against God:

> *"In like manner also, that the women adorn themselves in modest apparel, with propriety and **moderation,** not with braided hair or gold or pearls or **costly clothing** but, which is proper for women professing godliness, with good works."*
> [1 Timothy 2:9-10]

Moderation in all things is what the scripture recommends when it comes to fashion; but in custom and culture, Jesus must be the standard of our living because He is the only way to heaven:

> *"Nor is there salvation in any other, for there is no other name under heaven given among men by which we must be saved."*
> [Acts 4:12]

Therefore, if you are still contributing to the family rituals or traditional religious celebrations, then you need to consider if you are acting contrary to God. You may need to repent and come back to Jesus Christ:

> *"Their sorrows shall be multiplied that hasten after another god: their drink offerings of blood will I not offer, nor take up their names into my lips."*
>
> *[Psalms 16:4]*

Also By The Author

Wilderness

ISBN 9781907971464

'Wilderness' is one of the most powerful books ever written on the subject of the wilderness experience. It is an invaluable book for believers who are aiming to stand firm in their Christian journey without wavering in faith.

It contains a deep revelation and provides comprehensive material for practising Christians who are facing challenges or oppression from their spiritual Enemy. It focuses on solutions here on earth and helps prepare God's children to reach their ultimate destination - God's city, the New Jerusalem.

Woman Warfare Weapon
ISBN 9781907971396

Looking at our world today, the hearts of many women are crying and asking for revenge. Many are wondering where it all went wrong and some allow bitterness, hatred and anger to fester in their minds because of the wounds they incurred from men during courtship or in marriage, and from fathers or father figures.

Some need deliverance from their darkened mind, sorrowful past and faulty foundation, caused by self-error, family background or deception from the chief priests of Satan.

Many women have been tied down and tormented under indescribable bondage and unbearable burdens like the Israelites in the land of Egypt. It's time for them to experience freedom and gain deliverance from witchcraft and the marine kingdom to enjoy the life that Jesus came to give in abundance [John 10:10].

Elijah: Prophet of Fire
ISBN 9789780808631

This book explains the power of God in action in the life of prophet Elijah. It reveals his exemplary ministry and guides the reader in exercising their God-given authority over the powers of darkness.

It presents fresh insights and proves that Jesus Christ is still at work just as in former times - *"Jesus Christ is same yesterday, today and forever"*.

Battle Cry Against Strongholds

This book is specially written to open the understanding of the children of God to the reality of the kingdom of darkness. The book is designed to lift up the ancient gates and everlasting doors which pave the way to breakthroughs. It is aimed at opening the prison doors for those in Satanic captivity so that they can walk free.

This book is targeted at releasing the possessions of the children of God held in the *"strong man's"* warehouse.

Crossing Your Jordan
ISBN 9789780808624

This book is an eye opener to every child of God about the activities of the enemy. It concentrates on issues relating to how the enemy operates invisibly and manifests himself visibly.

It is a concise, do-it-yourself collection of prayers, designed to be utilised in your own way for prompt deliverance and freedom from the enemy. Therefore, the book is a weapon of warfare and training artillery for every child of God seeking deliverance. It is also useful for those who simply desire to enhance their Christian prayer life.

Various Evangelical Tracts

All available from SSEO at their website:

www.sseooutreach.org.uk

www.ingramcontent.com/pod-product-compliance
Lightning Source LLC
Chambersburg PA
CBHW061643040426
42446CB00010B/1560